One-Minute Brainteasers

Alan Stillson

Sterling Publishing Co., Inc.
New York

For Gail
And our ever-supportive family

Edited by Jeanette Green

Mensa and the distinctive table logo are trademarks of
American Mensa, Ltd. (in the U.S.),
British Mensa, Ltd. (in the U.K.),
Australian Mensa, Inc. (in Australia),
and Mensa International Limited (in other countries)
and are used by permission.

Mensa as an organization does not express an opinion as being that
of Mensa or have any ideological, philosophical, political or religious
affiliations. Mensa specifically disclaims any responsibility for any
liability, loss or risk, personal or otherwise, which is incurred as a
consequence, directly or indirectly, of the use and application of any of
the contents of this book.

Library of Congress Cataloging-in-Publication Data Available

8   10   9

Published by Sterling Publishing Co., Inc.
387 Park Avenue South, New York, NY 10016
© 2001 by Alan Stillson
Distributed in Canada by Sterling Publishing
c/o Canadian Manda Group, 165 Dufferin Street,
Toronto, Ontario, Canada M6K 3H6
Distributed in Great Britain and Europe by Chris Lloyd at Orca Book
Services, Stanley House, Fleets Lane, Poole BH15 3AJ, England
Distributed in Australia by Capricorn Link (Australia) Pty. Ltd.
P.O. Box 704, Windsor, NSW 2756, Australia

Sterling ISBN 0-8069-0187-X

For information about custom editions, special sales, premium and
corporate purchases, please contact Sterling Special Sales
Department at 800-805-5489 or specialsales@sterlingpub.com.

CONTENTS

INTRODUCTION

One-Minute Brainteasers. It's an interesting title for an official American Mensa game book. Why one minute and why brainteasers?

Most puzzles in this book can be solved within a minute. This allows you, the busy thinker, to control and time your mental workouts. Every puzzle can be solved independently. You can begin and end wherever and whenever you wish. When you're ready for more exercise, simply pick up where you left off. Most puzzles here can be done without a pencil.

With a trivia question, you either remember the fact or you do not. A brainteaser coaxes a little thought; it teases you into constructs or concepts of your own. We like to think of it as a kind of breezy mental gymnastics that's great fun!

How easy or hard are these puzzles? Every brainteaser here was tested by a Mensa puzzle-testing panel. You can compare your results in solving each section with American Mensa members, people who have an I.Q. in the top 2 percent of the American population. Panel members solved about 65 percent of the puzzles correctly. Of course, results varied from one group of puzzles to another.

Some puzzles may have alternate solutions that we didn't think of. Evaluate your results accordingly.

This book is divided into five parts: "Quick Word Puzzles," "Something in Common," "Jargon," "What's in a Name," and "In Reverse." The fifth part, "In Reverse," is kid-friendly.

Ready to rev up your mental motor? Here's your green light.

Mensa Testing

Sixty-seven members of American Mensa, Ltd., volunteered to be members of the testing panel for *One-Minute Brainteasers.* They received the puzzles by e-mail with instructions to take no more than about a minute per puzzle, and they sent back their answers. We tabulated the results, rounding off the percentage of correct answers to the nearest 5 percent for each group of puzzles and for the whole book.

American Mensa Puzzle-Testing Panel

I'd like to give special thanks to members of the Mensa puzzle-testing panel for this book: Ilene Hartman-Abramson, Ph.D.; Bob Berreth; Nancy Beringer; Ginni Betts; Vince Bonzagni; Lucia M. Britton; Rick Brooks; Howard Bryks; Christian Burgasser; Jody Carlson; Jim Corbin; Darrell Costello; Penelope Crittenden; Ben Curtis; Mo Demers; Christine M. Dudlak; George Dunn; Helen D. Edersheim; Jonathan Elliott; Ted Elzinga; Devin Eyre; Tom Fagan; Barbara J. Fontaine; Rita Foudray; Thomas G. Funk; Ann Garbler; Pete Gouvitsas; Bob Heasley; Robert Heine; John T. Henderson; Eric Holmquist; David B. Horvath, CCP; Richard Horvitz; Edward H. Julius; David P. Keeser; Ronald M. Kupers; Steve Latterel; Linda Lavelle; David Linko; Elaine Loughrey; Lois Mason; Mike Mayer; John Mochan; Sandra J. Nelson; Frank Anthony Oblak; Kristina Olsen; Phil Randolph; Sandie Romans; Miriam Schneidmill; Larry Schwartz; Lisa Schwartz; David Shapiro; Scott Sheldon; Bill Siderski; Joseph A. Spadaro; Dirk Steinmeier; Barry J. Stone; Timothy J. Sullivan; Rachel L. Tanzer; Gregory P. Tenerowicz; A. S. Tepper; Bethany Thivierge; Richard Till; Billie L. Tolman; Selena Updegraff; Judy Whittaker; Andrea M. Williams; John Woodlock; Rachel Young.

We also want to thank two gifted children, Kyle and Ryan, for helping us test the kid-friendly puzzles.

About the Author

Alan Stillson's puzzles have appeared in *American Way*, the American Airlines in-flight magazine. He is puzzle editor for Greater Los Angeles Mensa and produces a local public television show on interactive puzzle-solving. His puzzle books *The Mensa Genius ABC Quiz Book* and *Match Wits with Mensa,* co-authored with Marvin Grosswirth and Dr. Abbie Salny, continue to delight readers. His puzzles have been reviewed in *People* magazine. Mr. Stillson is a member of Mensa, the National Puzzlers League, and the National Scrabble Association.

Part I

QUICK WORD PUZZLES

Answers are on pages 76–79.

Vowel Exchange

Find back-to-back words with the same number of letters that are spelled alike except for one vowel. Except for the vowel sound, the words are pronounced alike, unlike CODE and CEDE–*code* has a hard C (like "K") and *cede* a soft C (like "S"). We avoid multiple-vowel combinations, like GRIN GREEN. In parentheses is the number of letters of the desired words.

> After a vampire BAT BIT me, I needed rabies shots. (3)
> The restaurant bandits liked to ROB RIB joints. (3)
> The runner LOST LAST year's race. (4)

1 The poker player wanted to _____ _____ he was out of money. (3)

2 After seeing that it wasn't successful, the charity's board of directors decided to _____ _____ as a fund-raising tool. (5)

3 How often do the passengers on a cruise _____ _____ for bargains at local stores when they're at a port? (4)

4 The orchestra had a _____ _____ section. (6)

5 Ship hands raising a _____ _____ know exactly what they're doing. (4)

6 Do people in _____ _____ longer? (4)

7 The stock analyst expected to see manufacturers of the latest computer _____ _____ prices within six months. (4)

8 The _____ _____ skipped out of town before the medical board could find out he wasn't a real doctor. (5)

9 It's hard to watch sailors at a _____ _____ with their loved ones. (4)

10 Is there a handyman I can _____ _____ in the neighborhood? (4)

Vowel Exchange

11 They watched their ____ ____ a hole in the backyard. (3)

12 Prospectors looking for gold ____ ____ scattered throughout this area. (3)

13 People who like to ____ ____ for all kinds of excuses to justify their constant complaining. (5)

14 At the local police ____ ____ of off-duty officers is a major item in their personnel files. (10)

15 Coffee drinkers don't expect a ____ ____. (5)

16 After ____ ____ at the directors' meeting, Mr. Lee received a standing ovation. (5)

17 Did Mrs. O'Leary's cow really make the ____ ____ and start the Chicago fire? (4)

18 *Elite* is among the words that begin ____ ____ with the same vowel. (3)

19 Would a ____ ____ out for small aircraft while flying? (5)

20 The ____ ____ produce water only as clean as the river that feeds it. (4)

Answers are on page 76.

Rhyme Time

We can create sentences with rhyming words: "Don't FALL over the BALL in the HALL, PAUL." If you're given only the first one or more letters of the word or none at all, finding words that rhyme can be challenging. Consider this sentence:

"Garment manufacturers were GL____ to _____ to their coffers during the F____ to be CL____ in PL____."

The rhyming words *glad, add, fad, clad,* and *plaid* work to make a sensible sentence: "Garment manufacturers were GLAD to ADD to their coffers during the FAD to be CLAD in PLAID." Find the rhyming words that fit in the blanks.

1 Safety is a F____ when asking an _____ to fall from a TR____.

2 His last S____ with his shrink covered modes of EXPR____ of AGGR_____.

3 The farmer R____ his crops would be F___ the S____ time around.

4 Did Mr. Wright build a D____ H____ in R____ on sandy L_____?

5 It was her BEL____ that the period of GR____ following a tragedy should be BR____.

6 S____ saw a F____ on the L____ just before D____.

7 If OTH____ were more M____ he'd have been a happier F____.

8 WH____ KN____ Y____ FL____?

9 The G____ was eaten by a M____ on the L____.

10 They advised PER____ to G____ SL____.

Rhyme Time

11 The Lone Ranger told T____ he needed to get to TOR____ PR____.

12 The last time I played P____ a cigar SM____ kept getting the J____.

13 She was a firm BEL____ that having a Labrador RETR____ kept her from getting cabin F____.

14 What are the chances of getting SUKIY____ and R____ road ice cream at a H____ game?

15 The MAJ____ of executives with SENI____ are careful not to misuse their AUTH____.

16 The best chance for an ACQU____ is to WH____ away at the prosecution's case a L____ at a time.

17 The lecturer's T____ was how he became MY____ after crossing the TR____ of Capricorn.

18 The golfer started to ____ unprintable words when his P____ began to SP____.

19 The F____ C____ S____ ____ B____ Masterson's table.

20 The police officer caught the fleeing suspect in H____ terrain and knocked him S____ with a B____ club.

Answers are on page 77.

Broadway Shows

Most Broadway show titles are concise. The Broadway hit show *Rent* sounds better than the would-be description "Monthly Payment Written into a Contract between Lessee and Lessor." Fortunately, such language is suppressed by the playwright or producer's good sense. But what if it were not? Find the original titles for these shows.

1 *The Male of Maximum Degree of Contentment*

2 *Osculate with Me, Katherine*

3 *Automobile Lubrication Chemical*

4 *A Refrain with the Shortest Distance between Two Points*

5 *Mr. Presley's Nickname and Myself*

6 *Positive Tidings*

7 *Female of Ten Percent of a Decade*

8 *Setting of Nocturnal-Variety Entertainment and Imbibing*

9 *Condemn Northerners*

10 *Nocturnal Apparel Diversion*

Answers are on page 77.

Answers are on page 77.

MENSA SCORING

Average Mensa Score:	70%

Broadway Songs

Most Broadway song titles are concise. Figure out the original title from the pretentious version of the title below.

1 "Ascend the Complete Set of Precipices"

2 "Express Celestial Gratitude for the Existence of Young Females"

3 "In the Event That a Male First-Person Singular Had a Substantial Net Worth"

4 "The Involuntary Nocturnal Vision That Has a Zero Probability of Occurrence"

5 "Second-Person Singular Will, Under No Circumstance, Perambulate while Unaccompanied"

6 "First-Person Singular Had the Option to Engage in Waltzes, Fox Trots, et al. throughout the Complete Nocturnal Period"

7 "Randomness, Manifest Yourself as a Female"

8 "A Location Exists for the Specific Benefit of First-Person Plural"

9 "*Homo Sapiens* Will Verbalize Our Mutual Displays of Affection"

10 "Digital Storage Capacity"

Answers are on page 77.

MENSA SCORING	
Average Mensa Score:	70%

Buried Song Titles

A nonsense phrase may bury other words. UNSURFACED TENACITY, for example, hides the song title "SURF CITY" buried in the words "unSURFaced tenaCITY." Find the song titles in these nonsense phrases.

1 ENEMY HIDEAWAY

2 COLD UNMANAGEABLE DRIVERS

3 CONDOMINIUM COMPREHENSION COMMISSION

4 FORECLOSED PHOTOGENIC BAYOU

5 VALLEY VACATION

6 AIRBORNE ATOMS ENCUMBER WILDERNESS

7 STEAL COMFORTABLE FLATWORMS

8 CLOVES SUPPLEMENT WISDOM

9 WEATHER'S MOROSE

10 POISONOUS CURARE

Answers are on page 78.

Call Letters

North American radio and TV stations have three or four call letters. In general, U.S. stations east of the Mississippi River begin with *W*, those west of the Mississippi begin with *K*, those based in Canada begin with *C*, and those based in Mexico begin with *X*.

Using four call letters for imaginary stations, we can have fun matching the four-letter word that the call letters spell out with the station's format or motto. WHIM could be a TV station for impulsive watchers, CLOY a radio station that favors overly sweet and sticky music, and KITE a station for high fliers.

Create appropriate call letters for these would-be stations.

1 The station for Boy Scouts and Girl Scouts

2 The secretly super station

3 The station for hopeful listeners

4 The very end

5 The station that sees right through you

6 The indifferent station

7 The station for royalty

8 The station for chowderheads

9 The studying students' station

10 The Rosebud station

Answers are on page 78.

In each word puzzle below, some letters have been given. Fill in the letter blanks to make a word. Here are some examples.

C _ T T H _ _ _ _ T   CUTTHROAT
W _ _ _ _ Z   WALTZ
_ _ C H N _ Q _ _   TECHNIQUE

1   G _ _ B _ G _

2   O _ _ _ O X _ O _ _

3   _ U _ _ K _ _ Y

4   _ Y R R _

5   F _ A _ H _ _ _ _ H _

6   _ X Q _ _ S _ _ _ _

7   G _ _ R K _ _

8   C _ N C _ C _ _ _ _ N

9   _ B _ Q _ _ _ _ _ _

10   _ _ V _ _ V _ M _ _ _ _

Answers are on page 78.

Names & Initials

Once in a while, a person has a perfect first name and last-name initial for his or her field of expertise. For example, Travis T. would suit a lawyer who wins bad cases by exploiting loopholes. Curtis C. could write an etiquette column. Find the ideal first name and last-name initial to fit these fields of expertise.

1 A meticulous butler

2 An editor of a major newspaper

3 A writer of action-packed comic strips

4 A CEO of a major fabric-manufacturing company

5 An expert in negotiating international treaties

6 A London police officer

7 A commercial fisherman

8 A chronicler of Arabian folktales

9 A podiatrist

10 A honeydew grower

Answers are on page 79.

Answers are on page 79.

MENSA SCORING

Average Mensa Score:	30%

Common Interiors

Sometimes, two words have a common interior. For example, the interior letters of EARTH and PARTY are ART (eARTh, pARTy); inside EFFORT and AFFORD are the letters FFOR.

Find the common interiors of these word pairs.

1 C _ _ _ _ _ S & O _ _ _ _ _ _ T

2 C _ _ _ _ N & G _ _ _ _ L

3 O _ _ _ T & A _ _ _ D

4 J _ _ _ _ Y & R _ _ _ _ D

5 C _ _ _ _ B & B _ _ _ P

6 E _ _ H & B _ _ K

7 A _ _ _ N & F _ _ _ R

8 C _ _ _ _ E & M _ _ _ R

9 G _ _ _ T & P _ _ _ O

10 P _ _ _ E & C _ _ _ M

Answers are on page 79.

Repeaters

A few words in the English language begin with a letter or a combination of letters that's immediately repeated. Examples include AARDVARK, RERECORD, and MURMURING. Try to find "repeaters" that logically complete these sentences.

1 The green salad contained lettuce, celery, and _____.

2 The wind can make _____ sounds when it blows through canyons.

3 New software was used to produce those _____ graphics.

4 Will your trip to Italy include a _____ visit?

5 She had a nonspeaking part in "Conan the _____."

6 The room contained a futon and a _____ mat.

7 They drank pure red-orange _____ juice every day in Hawaii.

Most Chinese restaurants serve black _____ tea.

9 The _____ were ringing their bells.

10 The _____ of the end of the world has embarrassed many cult leaders.

Answers are on page 79.

Repeaters

11 Some people prefer a cup of hot _____ to coffee.

12 Some adults love to _____ the books they enjoyed during childhood.

13 The oil that's _____ onto the driveway will cause a stain.

14 The florist sold many roses and _____ last year.

15 Children often _____ their parents.

16 Sometimes, the best-lit room in the aquarium contains the _____.

17 It can be fascinating watching an insect emerge from its _____.

18 The vacation package includes a _____ ride near Macchu Picchu.

19 The con man promised that the investment would return _____ of money.

20 A piña colada typically contains blended rum, pineapple, and _____.

Answers are on page 79.

Answers are on page 79.

MENSA SCORING	
Average Mensa Score:	60%

Part II

SOMETHING IN COMMON

Answers are on pages 80–85.

Something in Common

Find what all the things in Column A have in common that none of the things in column B have in common. Here are two examples.

COLUMN A	COLUMN B
Glory	Practical
Sword	Yard
Marching	Drum
Coming	Patriotic
Grapes	Sit

All words in Column A are in "The Battle Hymn of the Republic."

COLUMN A	COLUMN B
Vacuum	Batter
Aardvark	Horror
Smooth	Inspired
Reed	Mangrove
Caboose	Deter

All words in Column A have consecutive double vowels.

There are many correct ways to state a solution. For instance, in the second example, it's valid to say, "The words in Column A have the same vowel back-to-back." Consider your answer correct if it states the right idea in any reasonable way. We include Column B to help eliminate answers that are technically correct, but trivial (such as words with less than fifteen letters).

We've arranged these puzzles in three sections—Miscellany (pages 23–29), Same-Size Words (pages 30–36), and Names & Places (pages 37–43). In each puzzle, find what all the items in Column A have in common that the items in Column B do not. We've also thrown in one bonus puzzle (#21) at the end of each section.

Answers are on pages 80–85.

Miscellany

1 COLUMN A   COLUMN B

COLUMN A	COLUMN B
Facade	Building
Rendezvous	Gum
Matinee	Steel
Pirouette	Order
Gauche	Algebra

2

COLUMN A	COLUMN B
Ghost	Culminate
Height	Habit
Honor	Apprehend
Spaghetti	Float
Psyche	Psalm

3

COLUMN A	COLUMN B
Insoluble	Inspire
Ineffective	Ingot
Indefinite	Incantation
Inarticulate	Injurious
Incapable	Interval

Answers are on page 80.

SOMETHING IN COMMON

Miscellany

4 COLUMN A   COLUMN B

Tapering   Ocean

Pious   Quinoa

Capitol   Educating

Devour   Columnar

Anxious   Mundane

5 COLUMN A   COLUMN B

Muscat   Carbon

Scattered   Fraction

Confiscate   Remember

Vacation   Float

Cathedral   Stacking

6 COLUMN A   COLUMN B

Awfully   Effective

Flower   Clown

Whereof   Excavate

Curfew   Festooned

Welfare   Nowhere

Answers are on page 80.

Miscellany

7 COLUMN A   COLUMN B

Emulate   Tricky

Dogma   Fixture

Catamaran   Bowling

Camellia   Castle

Boarding   Selfish

8 COLUMN A   COLUMN B

Popular   Election

Inundate   Lance

Llama   Ramrod

Diadem   Chronic

Tooth   Cheetah

9 COLUMN A   COLUMN B

Key   Part

Goose   Duck

Soon   Tangle

Oxide   Isle

Arch   Praise

SOMETHING IN COMMON

Answers are on page 81.

Miscellany

10 COLUMN A COLUMN B

COLUMN A	COLUMN B
Water	Emit
Nickel	Felt
Bill	Known
Wings	Oxygen
White	Present

11 COLUMN A COLUMN B

COLUMN A	COLUMN B
Gaze	Glaze
Crag	Big
Cage	Swing
Stagger	High
Goose	Clogged

12 COLUMN A COLUMN B

COLUMN A	COLUMN B
Amoeba	Each
Area	Canoe
Automate	Acetone
Idea	Idealist
Unique	Queue

Answers are on page 81.

Miscellany

13 COLUMN A   COLUMN B

COLUMN A	COLUMN B
Well	Water
Ice	Skin
Rip	Ruin
Angle	Army
River	Coal

14 COLUMN A   COLUMN B

COLUMN A	COLUMN B
Coast	Offer
Torture	Tension
Thumb	Pinky
Brittle	Vintage
Salvation	Yesterday

15 COLUMN A   COLUMN B

COLUMN A	COLUMN B
Piano	Apple
Game	Lost
Hunch	Most
Part	Greater
Record	Unique

Answers are on page 81.

SOMETHING IN COMMON

Miscellany

16 COLUMN A | COLUMN B

COLUMN A	COLUMN B
Embrace	Embarrass
Basic	Facade
Subtract	Ability
Cabinet	Invoke
Contraband	Beckoned

17 COLUMN A | COLUMN B

COLUMN A	COLUMN B
Mill	Stream
Compass	Push
On	Metal
Rat	Ivory
Quest	Dog

18 COLUMN A | COLUMN B

COLUMN A	COLUMN B
Corps	Brisk
Climb	Audit
Myrrh	Light
High	Exhaust
Hymn	Psalm

Answers are on page 81.

Miscellany

19 COLUMN A

Rate

Example

Rib

Number

Location

COLUMN B

Hum

Ironic

Thumb

Guild

Attic

20 COLUMN A

Portion

Role

Separate

Side

Section

COLUMN B

Innocent

Lecture

Apt

Slide

Mint

21 COLUMN A

Reread

Refinance

Repaint

Restock

Reinstate

COLUMN B **BONUS (Add to score)**

Rested

Retrospect

Remnant

Reptile

Reality

MENSA SCORING	
Average Mensa Score:	45%

Answers are on page 82.

Same-Size Words

1 COLUMN A   COLUMN B

Spring	Huddle
Grants	Injure
Whilst	Booths
Length	Return
Prowls	Clinic

2 COLUMN A   COLUMN B

Flat	Hint
Ring	Knit
Inch	Ever
Glow	Bank
Tape	Cent

3 COLUMN A   COLUMN B

Sheds	Plate
Wedge	Acute
Young	Forms
Merge	There
Usury	Cloud

Answers are on page 82.

Same-Size Words

4 COLUMN A   COLUMN B

Sell   Part

Tine   Onyx

Seer   More

Rite   Mist

Bran   Fail

5 COLUMN A   COLUMN B

Fathers   Freight

Bittern   Muskrat

Acetone   Bemused

Furlong   Garbage

Carpets   Western

6 COLUMN A   COLUMN B

Pin   Pie

Mar   Dog

Tea   Arm

Sac   His

Too   You

Answers are on page 82.

SOMETHING IN COMMON

Same-Size Words

7 COLUMN A   COLUMN B

COLUMN A	COLUMN B
Image	Draft
Canoe	Aorta
Defer	Angst
Alone	Strap
Talon	Idiom

8 COLUMN A   COLUMN B

COLUMN A	COLUMN B
Broken	Theory
Narrow	Moment
Bottom	Eyeing
Subway	Papaya
Picket	Crutch

9 COLUMN A   COLUMN B

COLUMN A	COLUMN B
Ride	Yell
Fall	Joke
Will	Army
Time	Gull
Pass	Each

Answers are on page 82.

Same-Size Words

10 COLUMN A COLUMN B

Mica Puce

Tune Lily

Ties Bark

Gets Isle

Aged Papa

11 COLUMN A COLUMN B

Holly Sound

Month Amuse

Cream Grasp

Width Hatch

Defer Knoll

12 COLUMN A COLUMN B

Grave Grown

Gripe Grind

Great Gruel

Grass Grasp

Grill Grade

Answers are on page 83.

SOMETHING IN COMMON

Same-Size Words

13 COLUMN A   COLUMN B

Wit   Dim

Ran   Ore

Hat   Are

Pea   Hot

Par   Air

14 COLUMN A   COLUMN B

Boar   They

Card   Node

Rice   Hymn

West   Only

Ride   Calm

15 COLUMN A   COLUMN B

Verb   Most

Here   Flag

Opts   Jazz

Rift   Knit

Ores   Foal

Answers are on page 83.

Same-Size Words

16 COLUMN A

Garb
Aver
Host
Mile
Band

COLUMN B

Whim
Melt
Salt
Unto
Neon

17 COLUMN A

Woman
Mouse
Goose
Index
Annex

COLUMN B

Scale
Throw
Enter
Quail
Boxer

18 COLUMN A

Jab
Big
Fed
Ice
Had

COLUMN B

Toe
Cob
Pun
Leg
Ask

Answers are on page 83.

SOMETHING IN COMMON

Same-Size Words

19 COLUMN A   COLUMN B

COLUMN A	COLUMN B
Iron	Here
Bell	Born
Hand	Mine
Earl	King
Pink	True

20 COLUMN A   COLUMN B

COLUMN A	COLUMN B
Mend	Plan
Back	Duck
Pace	Ever
Mass	Push
Toll	Four

21 COLUMN A   COLUMN B **BONUS (Add to score)**

COLUMN A	COLUMN B
Mite	Zone
Rite	Kite
Taut	Tout
Wade	Hare
Site	Beet

MENSA SCORING   *Answers are on page 83.*

Average Mensa Score:	35%

Names & Places

1 COLUMN A   COLUMN B

Easter Island   New Zealand

South Korea   Rhode Island

Mount Sinai   South Dakota

Lake Mead   Bering Sea

Central America   Lake Tahoe

2 COLUMN A   COLUMN B

Firestone   Churchill

Wartenburg   Rhodes

Atwood   Samuels

Balfour   Ehrlich

Guthree   Thatcher

3 COLUMN A   COLUMN B

Norman, OK   Muskogee, OK

Storrs, CT   Waterbury, CT

Athens, GA   Macon, GA

Lawrence, KS   Liberal, KS

Tucson, AZ   Flagstaff, AZ

Answers are on page 84.

SOMETHING IN COMMON

Names & Places

4 COLUMN A

Empire State Building

Eiffel Tower

Parthenon

Space Needle

Wailing Wall

COLUMN B

Pyramid of Cheops

Colossus of Rhodes

Stonehenge

Shrine at Lourdes

Mount Rushmore

5 COLUMN A

Dubuque

Houston

Honolulu

Huntsville

Albuquerque

COLUMN B

Minneapolis

Tacoma

Miami

Salt Lake City

Dallas

6 COLUMN A

La Bohême

The Marriage of Figaro

William Tell

Tristan und Isolde

Carmen

COLUMN B

The Messiah

The Surprise Symphony

Eine Kleine Nachtmusik

The 1812 Overture

Ave Maria

Answers are on page 84.

Names & Places

7

COLUMN A	COLUMN B
Cooper	Jones
Goldschmidt	Jamison
Smith	McMahon
Harper	Lee
Granger	Brown

8

COLUMN A	COLUMN B
Arizona	California
Indiana	New York
Massachusetts	Florida
Utah	New Mexico
Arkansas	Wisconsin

9

COLUMN A	COLUMN B
The Big O	Hammerin' Hank
Magic	Broadway Joe
Pistol Pete	Mister October
Doctor J	The Greatest
The Stilt	Charley Hustle

Answers are on page 84.

SOMETHING IN COMMON

Names & Places

10 COLUMN A

Volare

Autumn Leaves

The Happy Wanderer

C'est Si Bon

More

COLUMN B

The Wayward Wind

All the Way

Maria

Your Cheatin' Heart

She Loves You

11 COLUMN A

Royal Crown

Doctor Brown

Canada Dry

A&W

Barq's

COLUMN B

Pampers

Zenith

Lipton

Campbell's

Kodak

12 COLUMN A

Carousel

Paint Your Wagon

Ragtime

Show Boat

West Side Story

COLUMN B

Evita

The King and I

Gigi

Camelot

Fiddler on the Roof

Answers are on page 84.

Names & Places

13 COLUMN A

San Jose

Philadelphia

Columbus

Buffalo

Dallas

COLUMN B

Cleveland

San Francisco

Albuquerque

Oklahoma City

New Orleans

14 COLUMN A

Cool Hand Luke

Hud

Exodus

The Hustler

Cat on a Hot Tin Roof

COLUMN B

The Way We Were

It's a Wonderful Life

The Ten Commandments

Love Story

Giant

15 COLUMN A

Aspen, CO

Sun Valley, ID

Park City, UT

Lake Placid, NY

Squaw Valley, CA

COLUMN B

Honolulu, HI

Palm Springs, CA

Daytona Beach, FL

Hilton Head, SC

Lubbock, TX

Answers are on page 85.

Names & Places

16 COLUMN A

So in Love

Night and Day

I Love Paris

Anything Goes

True Love

COLUMN B

Over There

Michelle

Mammy

Old Man River

April in Paris

17 COLUMN A

Helene

Charlotte

Betty

Suzette

Melba

COLUMN B

Martina

Jill

Mercedes

Hillary

Diane

18 COLUMN A

Muncie

Vincennes

Logansport

Evansville

Valparaiso

COLUMN B

Schenectady

Cape May

Raton

Yuma

Mankato

Answers are on page 85.

Names & Places

19 COLUMN A   COLUMN B

COLUMN A	COLUMN B
Murphy	Jones
Busch	Kelly
Comiskey	Rizzo
Jacobs	Presley
Ebbets	Thorpe

20

COLUMN A	COLUMN B
Corpus Christi	Fresno
Providence	Salt Lake City
Los Angeles	Houston
St. Petersburg	Fort Lauderdale
New Canaan	Columbus

21

COLUMN A	COLUMN B **BONUS (Add to score)**
The African Queen	Gone with the Wind
The Maltese Falcon	Oklahoma
To Have and Have Not	The Magnificent Seven
The Big Sleep	Double Indemnity
Key Largo	Run Silent Run Deep

SOMETHING IN COMMON

MENSA SCORING   *Answers are on page 85.*

Average Mensa Score:	45%

Crazy Z (Bonus)

These sentences all contain words with one or more Z's in them. Find words or names with the crazy Z's that make sense in the sentence. Here's an example: The barber said, "I'll cut that hair down to _ _ Z _" and gave me a _ _ ZZ cut. The missing Z words are *SIZE* and *BUZZ*.

1 Mom took a pepperoni _ _ Z Z _ out of the _ _ _ _ Z _ _.

2 Despite the _ _ _ _ _ Z, the quarterback got the ball to his receiver in the end Z _ _ _.

3 If you back up your data on a Z _ _ drive, there's a Z _ _ _ chance that any of it will be lost.

4 I was too _ _ Z _ to go to the Z _ _ today.

5 The video-game player tried to Z _ _ a _ _ Z _ _ bad guys with his laser beam.

6 I learned about former Presidents like John _ _ _ Z _ _ _ _ _ _ _ Kennedy and Z _ _ _ _ _ _ _ Taylor.

7 Witch _ _ Z _ _ never _ _ Z _ _ off while she was flying on her broom.

8 Cleaning the _ _ Z _ after an oil spill can be a safety _ _ Z _ _ _.

9 _ _ _ Z _ _ is in South America and _ _ Z _ _ _ _ _ _ _ is in Africa.

10 It was too _ _ Z _ outside to _ _ Z _ at the mountains.

MENSA SCORING	*Answers are on page 85.*
Average Mensa Bonus Score:	85%
Average Mensa Score (Kids):	75%

Part III

JARGON

Answers are on pages 86–88.

Sporting Examples

In Part III, we play with *jargon*, a specialized vocabulary for a particular profession, and other topic-specific words to fill the blanks of sentence puzzles. Missing words allude to the topic at hand. We've included puzzles with words from food and the culinary arts, automotive matters, household items, and computer talk.

Just to prove we're good sports, we'll give you a few in sports jargon. Ready, guys and gals? Warm up with these examples before you play ball.

She read Euripides and _____ in Greek.
Solution: homer (Homer)

His favorite desserts _____ _____ pie and strawberry shortcake.
Solution: archery (are cherry)

Pillow factory workers often _____ _____.
Solution: touchdown (touch down)

Do students who major in poli _____ _____ to each other more than those who major in phys ed?
Solution: cycling (sci cling)

Got it? Give these puzzles on pages 47–64 your best *shot, put* down your answers, and *track* your results. (shotput, track)

Food Words

The sentence "Is _____ the list of the top ten Italian tourist cities?" can be completed with a food word, VENISON (Venice on). The sentence "They would not _____ _____ inside without our press credentials" can be completed with LETTUCE (let us). You may remember the old riddle about not starving in the desert because of all the SANDWICH is there. Find a food word to complete these sentences.

1 If we _____ this year, let's have a formal wedding next year.

2 Her only living relatives are a sister in Boston and _____ in Newark.

3 Mr. Mineo's agent said, "Let _____ some of his own dialogue."

4 The division that suffered the biggest budget _____ half their staff go.

5 If the loggers keep up the current _____ clearance in this section will be completed in three weeks.

6 Did an obsessed fan ever try to _____ Nova singer Astrud Gilberto?

7 If everybody would _____ or a dime more into the economy every day, there would be more employment.

8 When the ratings on her show _____ Tyler Moore formed a production company.

9 The line drive down the third base line landed _____.

10 They loved to watch Fred and _____ dance.

Answers are on page 86.

JARGON

Food Words

11 The witness saw the _____ up to the victim and stab him.

12 The dog tried to _____ his bone.

13 At the end of his contract _____ Estrada decided not to do any more episodes of "Chips."

14 Her grandparents used to always give up meat from _____ Easter Sunday.

15 Do all Wal-Mart executives have a portrait of _____ the wall in their offices?

16 Mr. and Mrs. Sampras once said, "_____ sure bet to become a top tennis player."

17 Even though Tom Hanks often acts like a _____ Ryan enjoys co-starring with him.

18 The choice was to stay in the air-conditioned room or to _____ the hot sun outside.

19 If Rocky Balboa saw Alice B. Toklas's significant other, he'd probably yell, "_____!"

20 She was too young to remember _____ Jeff.

Answers are on page 86.

Answers are on page 86.

MENSA SCORING

Average Mensa Score:	65%

Automotive Words

The sentence "If the hatchet is too small, the _____ get the job done" can be completed with a car-related word or name–*axle* (ax'll). "The Scrabble® player got a good score by placing an _____ a triple letter square" can be completed with *Exxon* (*X* on). Try to find a car-related word or name for these sentences.

1 The home video of the children running the hundred-yard _____ them to tears.

2 Why _____ be the only freeze-dried orange juice product that this store sells?

3 Most trombones have slides, but some have _____.

4 They drove from Cannes to _____ their French Riviera honeymoon.

5 It takes a lot of selling off of stocks to _____ market into a bear market.

6 Did a realtor negotiate the sale of the _____ Chemical Company bought for its largest factory?

7 The merchant hoped that most of the sailors in the _____ be regular customers when they came back to their homeport.

8 Movie fans watched Richard _____ from being a heartthrob in *Pretty Woman* to being a villain in *Nowhere to Hide*.

9 Travel guides usually _____ rates for the hotels they describe.

10 Did _____ Larry and Curly a lot of stories?

Answers are on page 87.

Automotive Words

11 At news conferences, politicians tend to _____ difficult questions.

12 It's difficult for accountants to take long _____ during tax season.

13 At the directors' convention, some people heard Federico Fellini and Carlo _____ all night long about their past accomplishments.

14 The poker player stayed in the pot with only an ace _____ too long.

15 Will the rancher to whom you sold the diseased _____ your neck when he finds out the truth?

16 The more conservative horse racing gambler might say, "When you're at the _____ the long shots and just bet on the favorites."

17 Frank Sinatra sang, "When I was seventeen, it was a very _____."

18 Can a salesperson who is _____ as well as one who is wordy?

19 Did her Siamese _____ hole in her sweater when he scratched it?

20 I don't want to hear another _____ story.

Answers are on page 87.

MENSA SCORING

Average Mensa Score:	50%

Household Items

The sentence "Would the field-goal kicker with the golden _____ up as much excitement as the quarterback with the golden arm?" can be completed with a word or name in household item jargon—*toaster* (toe stir). The sentence "_____ es su casa" can be completed with *Mikasa* (Mi casa). Try to find a household item (word or name) to complete these sentences.

1 The programmer working on the data _____ to finish the job in three weeks, but it ended up taking a full month.

2 A fan had called _____ few days earlier, but Mr. Piazza never got the message.

3 How was Ezekiel able to _____ from a prophecy?

4 Did Mama _____ the table when the Mamas and the Papas met for dinner?

5 At a large picnic, all the sandwiches had better _____ giving them out will take too much time.

6 When I put my money into a savings account, _____ interest.

7 Some historians think that because Nixon and Agnew got into hot _____ and Dole lost the election to Carter and Mondale.

8 Are reruns of "Starsky and _____" shown on any TV stations?

9 The student thought the final exam meant _____ or swim.

10 The bank has an armed _____ all its branches.

Answers are on page 87.

Household Items

3

11 If we both had the same pet birds, would _____ to your crow?

12 The supermarket promotion limited quantities to one Easter _____ customer.

13 During the wedding ceremony, the bride said, "I will love this _____ the day I die."

14 The royal physician had to _____ Lancelot's wounds after his recent skirmish.

15 When you take the dog for a ride in the _____ her a few times and she'll settle down.

16 If the Lone Ranger got his horse into the Kentucky Derby, would _____ the garland of roses at the end of the race?

17 A well-known palindrome goes, "_____ plan, a canal— Panama."

18 Well, then how about reruns of "Hunter" starring Fred _____?

19 A fielder _____ the runner or throw the ball to the proper base for a force-out.

20 The special teams coach had the right to _____ kickers and punters.

Answers are on page 87.

MENSA SCORING	
Average Mensa Score:	55%

Computer Talk

The sentence "The boxing champion faced many challengers, but he _____ all down" can be completed with a word in computer jargon–*modem* (mowed 'em). The sentence "Don't ever _____ I'll wash out your mouth with soap and water" can be completed with *cursor* (curse or). Try to find a word in computer jargon to complete these sentences.

1 Were both father and _____ when they fell asleep at the play last night?

2 After the first inning, the Yankees were ahead one _____.

3 Was Jack _____ a perfect 20–20 when he starred in "Dragnet"?

4 Did the new fishing _____ as well as the old one?

5 A male ovine is more commonly called a _____.

6 How often did Nikita speak to _____ the red phone?

7 The soldiers who were supposed to protect the _____ away instead.

8 Her favorite disaster movie was "Krakatoa East of _____."

9 The Ambassador will be _____ Aviv all of next week.

10 The Irish musician said, "Happiness is a _____ to eat and three or four groupies."

Answers are on page 88.

JARGON

Computer Talk

11 Charles didn't like to be called _____.

12 Rather than risk his next season being a _____ Wee Reese retired from baseball.

13 It's a long _____ from New York to Miami.

14 Does the wooden _____ twice as much as the aluminum one?

15 The city council decided to take _____ school funding issues at the next session.

16 There was a new challenge _____ Dillon during every episode of "Gunsmoke."

17 He tried reading the latest best-seller, but he just couldn't get _____.

18 There were no cold cuts in the refrigerator, so he opened a can of _____.

19 The shirts are available in S, M, L, and _____.

20 _____ a sorrowful thing to realize how few people appreciate Shakespearean English.

Answers are on page 88.

MENSA SCORING

Average Mensa Sscore:	55%

Part IV

WHAT'S IN A NAME?

Answers are on pages 89–92.

World Capitals

The sentence "Some of Mr. Preminger's friends wanted to throw _____ surprise party" can be completed with the name of a world capital–*Ottawa* (Otto a). The sentence "She fancied herself a blend of Gypsy Rose _____ Barker and Mata Hari" can be completed with *Lima* (Lee, Ma). Find a world capital to complete these sentences.

1 Many years ago, we saw George Burns joking with Milton _____ the Friar's Club.

2 That would make _____ years old and Mama seventy-six years old.

3 The driver was the _____ survivor of the crash.

4 _____ be the only catcher who had a cartoon bear named after him?

5 _____ Moffo and Kathleen Battle made the critic's list of the ten all-time best sopranos?

6 Did the customer with the silk paisley _____ for it before he left the store?

7 Smart merchants _____ improvement stores with many brands of tools.

8 After her marriages to Richard Burton, how many times has _____ divorced?

9 There was a Santa Claus suit in the shopping _____ brought home a few days before Christmas.

10 Is _____ the top-ten list of mantras?

Answers are on page 89.

World Capitals

11 A commercial machine should be capable of _____ after ton of dirty clothing.

12 The medium claimed to be able to communicate with the ghost of Marilyn _____ her seances.

13 Is _____ the widest shoe that's sold here?

14 Some spouses are faithful, but others _____.

15 If a police officer catches you making _____ is almost certain to follow.

16 Did one of Ms. Tucker's fans actually give _____ diamond ring?

17 What's a fair price for 100 one-third cut legal-size _____ file folders?

18 Sometimes the captain has to _____ ship in choppy waters.

19 The veteran of the Korean _____ many of his buddies get killed.

20 The dentist thought that if the plaque could be kept at _____ canal work could be avoided.

Answers are on page 89.

WHAT'S IN A NAME?

Each of the fifty states in the U.S. is presented here with two questions. Fill in the blank with the name of a city in the state mentioned.

Do you know how many _____ Evans got after falling off her horse in New York?   Scarsdale (scars Dale)
Were many SAT scores above the _____ Oklahoma?
Norman (norm in)

Find a one-word city or town in the state that completes the two questions for each of the fifty states.

1 How many _____ Ward stores were in Alabama?

2 Did the insurance salesman try to _____ and Pa a new policy in Alabama?

3 Is it legal to use a _____ de plume in Alaska?

4 Did a member of Steely _____ any treasure in Connecticut?

5 Was "The White Cliffs of _____" recorded in Delaware?

6 Was it appropriate to let the lawyers for Paula _____ so deep into Bill Clinton's past in Arkansas?

7 Is it true that _____ allowed to enter a guy's rest room in Arizona?

8 Was the _____ paid for a local paper a fair price in Arizona?

9 Can an automobile collector buy a _____ Torme once owned in California?

10 Was 3Com Stadium Dusty _____ of choice in California?

Answers are on page 90.

Cities & States

11 Can a brave person act even _____ in Colorado?

12 Do most restaurants give you a twist of _____ your Perrier in Colorado?

13 At what time of year is the ice so thin you can neither skate _____ safely in Connecticut?

14 Do people who want to get married in _____ they need to book a catering hall well in advance in Alaska?

15 Do local residents _____ to build a Presidential library in Arkansas?

16 Do tennis players get upset when they _____ in Delaware?

17 If a songwriter _____ jingle for Pepsi, will he or she become rich and famous in Florida?

18 Would an updated version of the parting of the Red _____ more tourists into Universal Studios in Florida?

19 Was she really _____ a lot of money or just talkin' a lot of nonsense in Georgia?

20 Is _____ hot month in Georgia?

Answers are on page 90.

Cities & States

21   _____ hotel be allowed to overbook rooms in Hawaii?

22   Does anybody know _____ Dee and Elton John never performed a duet in Hawaii?

23   Do children's shoe stores carry all the widths from a girl's triple A to a _____ in Idaho?

24   Is it true that after the war in _____ returned to Ma and the kids in Idaho?

25   Did _____ back too far in his chair and fall on Curly in Illinois?

26   Did Lerner and Lowe write "The Night They Invented _____" in Illinois?

27   Is parental consent required for sixteen year olds to _____ Indiana?

28   Was the _____ Moore Show seen by many people in Indiana?

29   How often do goal-setting executives achieve their _____ in Iowa?

30   Is a _____ usually surrounded by love seats in Iowa?

Answers are on page 90.

60

Cities & States

31 Are shoppers allowed _____ long time in store windows in Kansas?

32 Do voters tend to be _____ in Kansas?

33 Are there any volcanoesin Kentucky, and, if so, where would the volcanic _____ after an eruption?

34 Has _____ Henderson ever starred in *The Sound of Music* in Kentucky?

35 Are _____ cheese croissants heavily spiced in Louisiana?

36 Do history students learn about the _____ Doctrine in Louisiana?

37 Did the firecracker go _____ did it fail to explode in Maine?

38 Has a Beatles fan ever shaken hands with Lennon _____ in Maine?

39 Do you think _____ still put on teachers' desks in Maryland?

40 Do houses face _____ often than east in Maryland?

Answers are on page 90.

Cities & States

41 Did William Randolph ever say "I _____" in Massachusetts?

42 Do I have to repeat myself over _____ again in Massachusetts?

43 Would Batman be able to live as Bruce _____ in Michigan?

44 Have there been any fallow _____ in Michigan?

45 Was "The Jack Benny Show" with Don Wilson, Dennis Day, and _____ popular in Minnesota?

46 Did anybody care what kind of _____ Kaelin was in Minnesota?

47 Do you think that hitting a shot off the _____ be a good reason to break a golf club in Mississippi?

48 Can you open a game of draw poker with a pair of _____ Mississippi?

49 Did Janis _____ ever do a concert in Missouri?

50 Do people try to transfer property _____ names to avoid taxes in Missouri?

Answers are on page 91.

Cities & States

51 Did Ms. Keller's relatives try to find _____ place to live in Montana?

52 Do doctors use bookkeeping services to handle their _____ in Montana?

53 Are there books about anthropology and the search for the missing _____ Nebraska?

54 Is it true that with proper medical _____ injuries can be successfully treated in Nebraska?

55 Do students learn about Ulysses S. Grant and Robert _____ in Nevada?

56 Did Skitch _____ and the Tonight Show Band ever play in Nevada?

57 Do many people know what kind of _____ Arthur was in everyday life in New Hampshire?

58 Is there any place to land a _____ Jet in New Hampshire?

59 Was Senator Lott simply called _____ New Jersey?

60 Would a latter-day Noah ever try to build a _____ in New Jersey?

Answers are on page 91.

WHAT'S IN A NAME?

Cities & States

61 Would an arrested thug _____ his buddies in New Mexico?

62 Do many people participate in the _____ Poll in New Mexico?

63 Are _____ Goodman's recordings available in music stores in New York?

64 If _____ man off, is he likely to try to get back at you in New York?

65 Which bakery sells the best _____ Russe in North Carolina?

66 Is it true that the Mad _____ the most popular *Alice in Wonderland* character in North Carolina?

67 Do the production people in show _____ down many good shoot sites when they're in North Dakota?

68 Did Green Bay quarterback Brett _____ to school in North Dakota?

69 Is it easy for high school seniors to find a prom _____ Ohio?

70 Did Elmer Gantry ever deliver any of his _____ Ohio?

Answers are on page 91.

Cities & States

71 Did anybody besides Ms. Field see what _____ in Oklahoma?

72 Is it customary to _____ person in trouble in Oklahoma?

73 Can ships from a foreign _____ in Oregon?

74 Do government employees often _____ the rules in granting building permits in Oregon?

75 When should I tell _____ will be going to visit her mother in Pennsylvania?

76 Do winds most often blow in from the _____ Pennsylvania?

77 Is a _____ going to be needed to handle the next generation of cargo ships in Rhode Island?

78 Did the _____ Trio ever play in Rhode Island?

79 Would a solid marble _____ typical architectural feature in mansions in South Carolina?

80 Would a _____ more on a prison scale than on a home scale in South Carolina?

Answers are on page 91.

WHAT'S IN A NAME?

Cities & States

81 Can one find a good Bartlett or Bosc _____ in South Dakota?

82 Did the Chad _____ Trio ever perform in South Dakota?

83 How can horse racing be a _____ if there are no monarchs in Tennessee?

84 Do oldies stations still play "The _____ Stomp" in Tennessee?

85 Is it better to use _____ linoleum on kitchen floors in Texas?

86 How did the _____ Powers movies do in Texas?

87 Are there any celebrations of the day of the _____ equinox in Utah?

88 Did _____ Nash ever recite "Candy Is Dandy" in Utah?

89 Can a pilot who's in a _____ safely in Vermont?

90 Is there a safe place to _____ my goods when I'm in Vermont?

Answers are on page 92.

91 Do office supply stores usually have _____ machine pricing in Virginia?

92 Is it easy for a tired person to get some _____ Virginia?

93 Do pet groomers usually find it difficult _____ long-haired dog in rainy weather in Washington?

94 Would anybody understand me if I _____ Arabic dialect in Washington?

95 Do many mothers spend time _____ their babies in old-fashioned carriages in West Virginia?

96 Do Boy Scouts spend much time _____ cans and other debris on the trails in West Virginia?

97 How quickly _____ close down an unsafe factory in Wisconsin?

98 Who played Oscar _____ in the revival of *The Odd Couple* in Wisconsin?

99 Would his _____ the two-step with his neighbor's daughter in Wyoming?

100 Can you imagine _____ and Dr. Zhivago all together in Wyoming?

Answers are on page 92.

WHAT'S IN A NAME?

MENSA SCORING	
Average Mensa Score:	65%

Name Games

Some people's first names can be used as words that name an animal or object or describe an action, object, event, or animal. These sentences contain both. *Tom* couldn't tell if he were eating a *tom* or a hen turkey. *Flo* was asked to "go with the *flow*."

These sentences begin with a name that's also used as a word later in the same sentence. The second word may be spelled the same way or appear as a *homonym* (a word that sounds the same but is spelled differently). Fill in the blanks with names and words that create good, sensible sentences.

1 _____ liked to use a hand-held _____ when he was making a speech.

2 _____ had just two days to learn a new Christmas _____.

3 _____ stayed home from school because her temperature _____ above 99° F.

4 _____ decided not to _____ a mask for Halloween.

5 _____ liked the lasagna, but his sister thought it was a _____ too spicy.

6 _____ took a trip to Yellowstone Park and the Medicine _____ mountains.

7 _____ learned that some people use "et _____" instead of "et cetera."

8 _____ was trying to memorize the _____ of Rights.

9 _____ and his parents went to an _____ museum.

10 _____ has an uncle who's a lawyer who likes to _____ people.

Answers are on page 92.

MENSA SCORING	
Average Mensa Bonus Score:	85%

Part V

IN REVERSE
Kid-Friendly Puzzles

Answers on pages 93–94

Reversible Words

Some words, when spelled backward, give us a different word. These aren't palindromes (like POP or SEES), and since they don't have a fancy name, we'll call them "reversible words." Examples are REWARD or DRAWER and ON or NO. The word REWARD when reversed spells DRAWER. The "reverse" of ON is NO. These sentences have reversible words:

The sheriff found an old REWARD poster in a dresser DRAWER. When the judge is seated ON the bench, there must be NO talking.

Fill the blanks in these sentences with reversible words (first spelled one way then in reverse) so that they make good sense.

1   _____ is as selfless as I _____.

2   There is a _____ of leftover stew on the _____ shelf of the refrigerator.

3   _____ is well-known that "_____" is the note after "la."

4   The beaver got _____ at animals that disturbed his _____.

5   I was so hungry that I ate my _____ sandwich on the _____.

6   Kittens are great _____ as long as you don't _____ on them.

7   I went to _____; then I dreamed about clowns tripping on banana _____.

8   The rock _____ kept mice and _____ as pets.

9   Sometimes a _____ of calamine lotion can soothe a _____ itch.

10 The _____ _____ not in the tool shed, where it belonged.

Answers are on page 93.

Reversible Words

11 The quick brown fox said, " _____ no!" as the riders yelled, "Tally _____!"

12 It's _____ to stay off ski lifts and _____ while they're being repaired.

13 The best _____ of the story was watching the hero _____ the spy.

14 There was some _____ stuck on Mom's coffee _____.

15 Yes, you _____ have another _____ after you finish your turkey.

16 The bully had no friends because he always tried to _____ his _____.

17 My aunts sometimes make a big _____ over who _____ a better sweater.

18 My Chihuahua is a great _____ so I let him sit on my _____.

19 We _____ about to study the _____ of the dinosaur.

20 After _____ tries, I finally served the ball over the _____.

Answers are on page 93.

Reversible Words

21 Dad wanted to _____ my paper about how the _____ is affected by the moon.

22 When my uncle is in a bad _____, he talks about gloom and _____.

23 I'd rather _____ for gold than take a _____.

24 There's a rumor that _____ people _____ in the old house.

25 The mail carrier was _____ by his boss for failure to _____ the mail on time.

26 A _____ that's heavier than air will _____ down to the bottom of a mineshaft.

27 Even a heavy television set does _____ weigh a _____.

28 He _____ yesterday but he's losing right _____.

29 Mom secured the bicycle _____ to the luggage rack with a thick _____.

30 If you think that silly mask will _____ anybody, you're _____.

Answers are on page 94.

Reversible Words

31 I didn't _____ washing the _____ until they were completely clean.

32 I _____ up my skates and took a speck of mud off the gold _____.

33 I'd never _____ a pet with _____ for one with fins.

34 I got a _____ that eating the inside of a peach _____ is bad for you.

35 My little brother plays with _____ toys, _____ I outgrew them.

36 Uranium can _____ a lot of radiation over a long period of _____.

37 If I _____ you on the shoulder, please pass me a _____ of butter.

38 I'm sure it's hard to train a _____ to push the _____ key.

39 You're more likely to find swimming _____ on an ocean liner than on a _____.

40 Sports-car owners like to _____ their _____ exhausts.

Answers are on page 94

Reversible Words

41 With these binoculars, you can _____ deer on the mountain _____.

42 That _____ of wind does nothing but _____ all the time.

43 That silly cat tried to _____ a bowling _____.

44 Some veterans of the Vietnam _____ still have _____ nerves.

45 I spilled some hair _____ on my left _____.

46 The sheriff wanted to _____ and feather the dirty _____.

47 Mom says it's a _____ to cook food in frying _____.

48 A boxer often _____ with his manager about how to _____ with his opponent.

49 The pilot had to find a _____ to adjust the _____ of the plane.

50 The condemned apartments _____ with every kind of vermin you can _____.

Answers are on page 94.

ANSWERS

Some puzzles may have alternate solutions that we didn't think of. Evaluate your results accordingly.

Part I

Quick Word Puzzles

ANSWERS

Vowel Exchanges **1**

1 BET BUT
2 SCRAP SCRIP
3 SHIP SHOP
4 STRONG STRING
5 MAST MUST
6 LOVE LIVE
7 CHIP CHOP
8 QUICK QUACK
9 PORT PART
10 HIRE HERE

Puzzles on page 8

Vowel Exchanges **1**

11 DOG DIG
12 ORE ARE
13 GRIPE GROPE
14 DEPARTMENT DEPORTMENT
15 BLAND BLEND *or* GRAND GRIND
16 SPIKE SPOKE
17 BARN BURN
18 AND END
19 WITCH WATCH
20 WELL WILL

Puzzles on page 9

Rhyme Time 2

1 factor actor tractor
2 session expression aggression
3 reckoned fecund second
4 dome home Rome loam
5 belief grief brief
6 Sean (Shawn) fawn lawn dawn
7 Othello mellow fellow
8 Who knew you flew?
9 goose moose loose
10 Perot go slow
Puzzles on page 10

Rhyme Time 2

11 Tonto Toronto pronto
12 poker smoker joker
13 believer retriever fever
14 sukiyaki rocky hockey
15 majority seniority authority
16 acquittal whittle little
17 topic myopic Tropic
18 utter putter sputter
19 fat cat sat at Bat
20 hilly silly billy

Puzzles on page 11

Broadway Shows 3

1 *The Most Happy Fella*
2 *Kiss Me, Kate*
3 *Grease*
4 *A Chorus Line*
5 *The King and I*
6 *Good News*
7 *Woman of the Year*
8 *Cabaret*
9 *Damn Yankees*
10 *Pajama Game*

Puzzles on page 12

Broadway Songs 4

1 "Climb Every Mountain"
2 "Thank Heaven for Little Girls"
3 "If I Were a Rich Man"
4 "The Impossible Dream"
5 "You'll Never Walk Alone"
6 "I Could Have Danced All Night"
7 "Luck, Be a Lady"
8 "There's a Place for Us"
9 "People Will Say We're in Love"
10 "Memory"

Puzzles on page 13

Buried Song Titles 5

1 eneMY hideaWAY
2 cOLD unMANageable dRIVERs
3 conDOminium compREhension comMIssion
4 foreCLOSEd phoTOgenic baYOU
5 vALLEY vaCATion
6 airBORNe aTOms encumBEr WILDerness

Buried Song Titles 5

7 sTEAl comFORtable flaTWOrms
8 cLOVEs suppleMEnt wisDOm
9 weaTHEr's moROSE
10 poiSOnous cuRARE

Puzzles on page 14

Call Letters 6

1 CUBS, CAMP, *or* KNOT
2 KENT
3 WISH
4 WXYZ, CODA, *or* WRAP
5 XRAY
6 COLD
7 KING
8 CLAM *or* CORN
9 CRAM
10 KANE

Puzzles on page 15

Hangwords 7

1 GARBAGE
2 OBNOXIOUS
3 QUACKERY *or* QUIRK-ILY
4 MYRRH
5 FLASHLIGHT
6 EXQUISITE
7 GHERKIN
8 CONCOCTION
9 UBIQUITOUS
10 INVOLVEMENT *or* DEVOLVEMENT

Puzzles on page 16

Names & Initials 8

1 Ty D. *or* Val A.
2 Dale E. *or* Marge N.
3 Marv L. *or* Rob N.
4 Lynn N.
5 Al I., Bart R., *or* Nate O.
6 Bob E. *or* Bob B.
7 Sam N. *or* Skip R.
8 Gene E., Al E., *or* Jean E.
9 Cal S. *or* Tony L.
10 Mel N.

Puzzles on page 17

Common Interiors 9

1 cUTLAS and oUTLASt
2 cRAVEn and gRAVEl
3 oCTEt and aCTEd
4 jOCKEy and rOCKEd
5 cLIMb and bLIMp
6 eACh and bACk
7 aLIEn and fLIEr
8 cANOe and mANOr
9 gIANt and pIANo
10 pHASe and cHASm

Puzzles on page 18

Repeaters 10

1 CUCUMBER *or* ALFAL-FA
2 EERIE, SUSURROUS, *or* ULULATING
3 VIVID
4 PAPAL
5 BARBARIAN
6 TATAMI
7 PAPAYA
8 OOLONG
9 TINTINNABULATORS
10 NONOCCURRENCE

Puzzless on page 19

Repeaters 10

11 COCOA
12 REREAD
13 OOZED
14 LILIES
15 MIMIC
16 EELS
17 COCOON
18 LLAMA
19 OODLES
20 COCONUT

Puzzles on page 20

Part II

Something in Common

ANSWERS

Miscellany `1`

1 All words in Column A are of French origin.

2 All words in Column A contain a silent "h." (*Height*, of course, contains both a voiced and a silent "h.")

3 All words in Column A use *in-* as a prefix meaning "not."

Puzzles on page 23

Miscellany `1`

4 All words in Column A have vowels in alphabetical order.

5 All words in Column A have CAT buried in them.

6 All words in Column A have both an "f" and a "w."

Puzzles on page 24

Miscellany   1

7   All words in Column A begin with an animal.

8   All words in Column A have the same first and second consonant.

9   All words in Column A can be preceded with *mon-*.

Puzzles on page 25

Miscellany   1

10   All words in Column A form an expression with *buffalo*.

11   The "g" in all words in Column A can be replaced with an "m".

12   All words in Column A have two more vowels than consonants.

Puzzles on page 26

Miscellany   1

13   All words in Column A can be preceded with a "d".

14   All words in Column A can form a word with every other letter.
CoAsT (CAT)
ToRtUrE (TRUE)
ThUmB (TUB)
BrItTlE (BITE)
SaLvAtIoN (SLAIN)

15   All the words in Column A can be played.

Puzzles on page 27

Miscellany   1

16   All words in Column A have the letters "a", "b", and "c".

17   All words in Column A can be followed by *-ion* to create a new word:
MILLION, COMPASSION, ONION, RATION, QUESTION

18   All words in Column A end in a silent letter.

Puzzles on page 28

Miscellany **1**

19 All words in Column A can be preceded with the word *prime*.
20 All words in Column A are a definition of the word *part*.

21 BONUS All words in Column A use *re-* as a prefix.

Puzzles on page 29

Same-Size Words **2**

1 All the six-letter words in Column A have only one vowel.
2 All four-letter words in Column A are a type of worm.
3 All five-letter words in Column A begin with a buried pronoun.
SHEds, WEdge, YOUng, MErge, USury

Puzzles on page 30

Same-Size Words **2**

4 All the four-letter words in Column A can have a "w" inserted somewhere in the word: sWell, tWine, seWer, Write, braWn
5 All seven-letter words in Column A consist of a three-letter word followed by a four-letter word: FAThers, BITtern, ACEtone, FURlong, CARpets
6 All three-letter words in Column A can be followed by a "k": pinK, marK, teaK, sacK, tooK
Puzzles on page 31

Same-Size Words **2**

7 All five-letter words in Column A have two syllables.
8 All six-letter words in Column A can be followed by the word *line*.
9 All four-letter words in Column A can be preceded by the word *free*.

Puzzles on page 32

Same-Size Words 2

10 All four-letter words in Column A can be preceded by *for:* FORmica, FORtune, FORties, FORgets, FORaged
11 All the five-letter words in Column A can have the third letter deleted: holy, moth, cram, with, deer
12 All five-letter words in Column A can have the *gr* replaced by *p:* Pave, Pipe, Peat, Pass, Pill

Puzzles on page 33

Same-Size Words 2

13 All three-letter words in Column A can be followed by *ch:* witCH, ranCH, hatCH, peaCH, parCH
14 All four-letter words in Column A can be preceded by *wild.*
15 All four-letter words in Column A can be preceded by *ad:* ADverb, ADhere, ADopts, ADrift, ADores

Puzzles on page 34

Same-Size Words 2

16 All four-letter words in Column A can be followed with *age:* garbAGE, averAGE, hostAGE, mileAGE, bandAGE
17 All five-letter words in Column A have irregular plurals (something other than *s*).
18 All three-letter words in Column A contain only the first ten letters of the alphabet (A–J).

Puzzles on page 35

Same-Size Words 2

19 All four-letter words in Column A can be followed by *y:* ironY, bellY, handY, earlY, pinkY
20 All four-letter words in Column A can be preceded by *a:* Amend, Aback, Apace, Amass, Atoll

21 BONUS All four-letter words in Column A have a homophone with a silent *gh:* miGHt, riGHt, tauGHt, weiGHed, siGHt

Puzzles on page 36

1   All places in Column A have the same number of letters in each word.

2   All names in column A have a buried number: FirestONE, WarTENburg, ATWOod, BalFOUR, GuTHREE

3   All cities and towns in Column A are home to a major state university.

Puzzles on page 37

4   All the tourist attractions in Column A are found in urban areas.

5   All cities in Column A contain at least one *u*.

6   All musican works in Column A are operas.

Puzzles on page 38

7   All surnames in Column A are derived from a form of work.

8   All states in Column A have state capitals with the largest city population in the state: Phoenix, Indianapolis, Boston, Salt Lake City, Little Rock

9   All the nicknames in Column A were given to basketball players.

Puzzles on page 39

10   All songs in Column A were originally written in a language other than English.

11   All brand names in Column A are for soda pop.

12   All musical shows in Column A are set in the United States.

Puzzles on page 40

Names & Places ![3]

13 All cities in Column A have National Hockey League teams.
14 All movies in Column A star Paul Newman.
15 All towns in Column A are ski resorts.

Puzzles on page 41

Names & Places ![3]

16 All songs in Column A were written by Cole Porter.
17 All female names in Column A have been associated with a dessert: pears helene, charlotte russe (fruit charlotte, etc.), apple betty (apple brown betty), crepe suzette, peach melba
18 All towns in Column A are in Indiana.

Puzzles on page 42

Names & Places ![3]

19 All surnames in Column A are or were names of a major-league baseball stadium.
20 All cities in Column A have names with a religious association.

21 BONUS All movies in Column A star Humphrey Bogart.

Puzzles on page 43

Crazy Z (Bonus) ![4]

1 pizza, freezer
2 blitz, zone
3 zip, zero
4 lazy, zoo
5 zap, dozen
6 Fitzgerald, Zachary
7 Hazel, dozed
8 ooze, hazard
9 Brazil, Mozambique
10 hazy, gaze

Bonus puzzles on page 44

Part III

Jargon

ANSWERS

Food Words   **1**

1   cantaloupe (can't elope)
2   anise (a niece)
3   salad (Sal add)
4   cutlet (cut let)
5   pastry (pace, tree) *or* pace (Pace)
6   kielbasa (kill bossa)
7   pumpernickel (pump a nickel)
8   rosemary (rose Mary)
9   fowl (foul)
10   ginger (Ginger)

Puzzles on page 47

Food Words   **1**

11   mango (man go)
12   berry (bury)
13   tumeric (term, Erik)
14   lentil (Lent til)
15   salmon (Sam on)
16   pizza (Pete's a)
17   nutmeg (nut, Meg)
18   bacon (bake in) *or* ham (ham)
19   yogurt ("Yo, Gert!")
20   mutton (Mutt &)

Puzzles on page 48

Automotive Words 2

1 dashboard (dash bored)
2 Mustang (must Tang)
3 valves
4 Nissan (Nice on)
5 convertible (convert a bull) *or* driveable (drive a bull)
6 Landau (land Dow)
7 Fleetwood (fleet would)
8 gearshift (Gere shift)
9 showroom (show room)
10 motel (Moe tell)

Puzzles on page 49

Puzzles on page 49

Automotive Words 2

11 Dodge (dodge)
12 brakes (breaks)
13 Pontiac (Ponti yak)
14 highway (high way)
15 steering (steer wring)
16 traction (track shun)
17 Goodyear (good year)
18 Tercel (terse sell)
19 Catera (cat tear a)
20 Saab (sob) *or* travel, road, or crank

Puzzles on page 50

Household Items 3

1 basement (base meant) *or* kneaded (needed)
2 formica (for Mike a)
3 television (tell a vision)
4 cassette (Cass set)
5 compactor (come packed or)
6 iron (I earn)
7 Waterford (water, Ford)
8 Hutch (hutch)
9 sink (sink)
10 garden (guard in)

Puzzles on page 51

Household Items 3

11 microwave (my crow wave)
12 hamper (ham per) *or* diaper (dye per)
13 mantle (man till)
14 dresser (dress Sir)
15 carpet (car, pet)
16 silverware (Silver wear)
17 Amana (A man a)
18 dryer (Dryer)
19 Maytag (may tag)
20 fireplace (fire place) *or* switch (switch)

Puzzles on page 52

JARGON ANSWERS

1   motherboard (mother bored)
2   zip (zip) *or* run (run)
3   website (Webb's sight)
4   network (net work) *or* net-cast (net cast)
5   RAM (ram)
6   icon (Ike on)
7   Fortran (fort ran)
8   Java (Java)
9   Intel (in Tel)
10   gigabyte (gig, a bite *or* jig, a bite) *or* byte (bite)

Puzzles on page 53

11   Chip (chip)
12   floppy (flop Pee)
13   drive (drive) *or* drag (drag)
14   Gateway (gate weigh)
15   upgrade (up grade)
16   format (for Matt)
17   Intuit (into it)
18   Spam (spam)
19   Excel (XL)
20   Lotus (Lo, 'tis)

Puzzles on page 54

Part IV

What's in a Name?

ANSWERS

World Capitals 1

1 Berlin (Berle in)
2 Papeete (Papa eighty)
3 Seoul (sole)
4 Canberra (Can Berra)
5 Havana (Have Anna)
6 Taipei (tie pay)
7 Stockholm (stock home)
8 Lisbon (Liz been)
9 Bahdad (bag Dad)
10 Amman (om on)

Puzzles on page 56

World Capitals 1

11 Washington (washing ton)
12 Monrovia (Monroe via)
13 Tripoli (triple E)
14 Rome (roam)
15 Bucharest (book, arrest)
16 Sofia (Sophie a)
17 Manila (manila)
18 Ankara (anchor a)
19 Warsaw (War saw)
20 Beirut (bay, root)

Puzzles on page 57

Cities & States 2

1 Montgomery
2 Selma (sell Ma)
3 Nome (nom)
4 Danbury (Dan bury)
5 Dover (Dover)
6 Jonesboro (Jones burrow)
7 Nogales (no gal is)
8 Buckeye (buck I)
9 Carmel (car Mel)
10 Bakersfield (Baker's field)

Puzzles on page 58

Cities & States 2

11 Boulder (bolder)
12 Limon (lime on)
13 Norwalk (nor walk)
14 Juneau (June know)
15 Hope (hope)
16 Lewes (lose)
17 Pensacola (pens a cola)
18 Sebring (Sea bring)
19 Macon (makin')
20 Augusta (August a)

Puzzles on page 59

Cities & States 2

21 Weimea (Why may a)
22 Waikiki (why Kiki)
23 Boise (boy's E)
24 Nampa ('Nam Pa)
25 Moline (Moe lean)
26 Champaine (Champagne)
27 Marion (marry in)
28 Gary (Garry)
29 Ames (aims)
30 Davenport (davenport)

Puzzles on page 60

Cities & States 2

31 Topeka (to peek a)
32 Liberal (liberal)
33 Ashland (ash land)
34 Florence (Florence)
35 Hammond (ham and)
36 Monroe (Monroe)
37 Bangor (bang or)
38 Orono (or Ono)
39 Annapolis (an apple is)
40 Westmore (west more)

Puzzles on page 61

Cities & States 2

41 Amherst (am Hearst)
42 Andover (and over)
43 Wayne (Wayne)
44 Dearborn (deer born)
45 Rochester (Rochester)
46 Mankato (man Kato)
47 Greenwood (green would)
48 Jackson (jacks in)
49 Joplin (Joplin)
50 Independence (in dependents')

Puzzles on page 62

Cities & States 2

51 Helena (Helen a)
52 Billings (billings)
53 Lincoln (link in)
54 Kearney (care knee)
55 Ely (E. Lee)
56 Henderson (Henderson)
57 Manchester (man Chester)
58 Concord (Concord)
59 Trenton (Trent in)
60 Newark (new ark)

Puzzles on page 63

Cities & States 2

61 Raton (rat on)
62 Gallup (Gallup)
63 Albany (all Benny)
64 Utica (you tick a)
65 Charlotte (Charlotte)
66 Hattaras (Hatter is)
67 Bismarck (biz mark)
68 Fargo (Favre go)
69 Dayton (date in)
70 Canton (cant in)

Puzzles on page 64

Cities & States 2

71 Sallisaw (Sally saw)
72 Ada (aid a)
73 Portland (port land)
74 Bend (bend)
75 Hershey (her she)
76 Easton (east in)
77 Newport (new port)
78 Kingston (Kingston)
79 Columbia (column be a)
80 Conway (con weigh)

Puzzles on page 65

WHAT'S IN A NAME? ANSWERS

Cities & States 2

81 Pierre (pear)
82 Mitchell (Mitchell)
83 Kingsport (king's sport)
84 Bristol (Bristol)
85 Tyler (tile or)
86 Austin (Austin)
87 Vernal (vernal)
88 Ogden (Ogden)
89 Rutland (rut land)
90 Stowe (stow)

Puzzles on page 66

Cities & States 2

91 Fairfax (fair fax)
92 Reston (rest in)
93 Tacoma (to comb a)
94 Spokane (spoke an)
95 Wheeling (wheeling)
96 Huntington (hunting tin)
97 Kenosha (can OSHA)
98 Madison (Madison)
99 Sundance (son dance)
100 Laramie (Lara, me)

Puzzles on page 67

Name Games 3

1   Mike, mike
2   Carol, carol
3   Rose, rose
4   Don, don
5   Tad, tad
6   Bo, Bow
7   Al, al.
8   Bill, Bill
9   Art, art
10 Sue, sue

Puzzles on page 68

Part V
IN REVERSE

Kid-Friendly Puzzles

ANSWERS

Reversible Words ▪

1 Ma, am
This sentence is a palindrome: It reads the same backward and forward.
2 pot, top
3 It, ti
4 mad, dam
5 sub, bus
6 pets, step
7 sleep, peels
8 star, rats
9 dab, bad
10 saw, was

Puzzles on page 70

Reversible Words ▪

11 Oh, Ho
12 smart, trams
13 part, trap
14 gum, mug
15 may, yam
16 slap, pals
17 stink, knits
18 pal, lap
19 are, era
20 ten, net

Puzzles on page 71

Reversible Words

21 edit, tide
22 mood, doom
23 pan, nap
24 evil, live
25 reviled, deliver
26 gas, sag
27 not, ton
28 won, now
29 parts, strap
30 stun, nuts

Puzzles on page 72

Reversible Words

31 stop, pots
32 laced, decal
33 swap, paws
34 tip, pit
35 tub, but
36 emit, time
37 tap, pat
38 bat, tab
39 pools, sloop
40 laud, dual

Puzzles on page 73

Reversible Words

41 spot, tops
42 bag, gab
43 nip, pin
44 War, raw
45 gel, leg
46 tar, rat
47 snap, pans
48 raps, spar
49 way, yaw
50 teem, meet

Puzzles on page 74

INDEX

Part titles and answer pages appear in boldface.

WHAT IS MENSA?

Mensa
The High IQ Society

Mensa is the international society for people with a high IQ. We have more than 100,000 members in over 40 countries worldwide.

Anyone with an IQ score in the top two percent of population is eligible to become a member of Mensa—are you the "one in 50" we've been looking for?

Mensa membership offers an excellent range of benefits:
• Networking and social activities nationally and around the world;
• Special Interest Groups (hundreds of chances to pursue your hobbies and interests—from art to zoology!);
• Monthly International Journal, national magazines, and regional newsletters;
• Local meetings—from game challenges to food and drink;
• National and international weekend gatherings and conferences;
• Intellectually stimulating lectures and seminars;
• Access to the worldwide SIGHT network for travelers and hosts.

For more information about American Mensa:
www.us.mensa.org
Telephone: (800) 66-MENSA
American Mensa Ltd.
1229 Corporate Drive West
Arlington, TX 76006-6103
USA

For more information about British Mensa (UK and Ireland):
www.mensa.org.uk
Telephone: +44 (0) 1902 772771
enquiries@mensa.org.uk
British Mensa Ltd.
St. John's House
St. John's Square
Wolverhampton WV2 4AH
United Kingdom

For more information about Mensa International:
www.mensa.org
Mensa International, 15 The Ivories, 6–8 Northampton Street, Islington, London N1 2HY, United Kingdom